Overcoming Anxiety: God's Promises

A Christian Guide to Overcoming Fear and Walking in God's Peace

Author

Written by: Pastor Tim Zapata

ACKNOWLEDGMENTS

I want to first and foremost thank my Lord and Savior Jesus Christ, for without Him, I am nothing. I also want to thank my wife, my partner, and my best friend, Pastor Rachel Zapata, for all the help and support she has given me and for believing in me when no one else did. Thank you, my love. I also want to thank my kids, Jordan, Josh, Bianca, and Jeseth, and their spouses. I also thank my grandkids, Emilia, Noah, Lydia, Amaris, Acalia, and Tobias, whom I love. I want to thank the Lord for my mom, who always prayed for me. I would not be where I am today if it weren't for her hard work and dedication to our family. My brothers and my sisters and their spouses, I love you. I want to thank my Victory Christian Center (VCC) family for trusting me and believing in the call that God placed in my life. Thank you to our pastors from VCC, Pastors Jose and Joann Zapata, and Saul and Stefani Cantu, for all your help and support.

Finally, I want to dedicate this book to my spiritual mother and mother-in-law, who has gone to be with the Lord, Pastor Lydia Garcia. She is the one who saw something in me that I didn't see in myself, and it is because of her that I am a pastor now. Thank you, Pastor Lydia, you will forever be in my thoughts. Thank you to all who helped make this book possible through your monetary donations and prayers. May the Lord bless you richly.

What is Anxiety? A Biblical Perspective

1. Introduction

2. Trusting in God's Sovereignty

3. Be Still and Know

4. Casting Your Cares

5. Guarding Your Heart and Mind

6. Renewing Your Mind

7. The Power of Praise

8. Living One Day at a Time

9. Walking in Faith, Not Fear

10. God's Promises in Times of Trouble

11. Breaking Free from the Spirit of Fear

12. Seeking God's Peace Daily

13. Encouragement Through Community

14. Victory Through the Word of God

15. Living in Freedom

16. Spiritual Warfare Against Anxiety

17. The Role of the Holy Spirit in Overcoming Anxiety

18. Prayers and Declarations for Anxiety-Free Living

19. Developing a Lifestyle of Trust

20. A Final Encouragement – Walking in God's Peace Permanently

Introduction

Purpose of the Book

Anxiety is a battle that many face in silence, often feeling as though they are alone in their struggles. This book was written to remind you that you are not alone, nor are you powerless in the face of anxiety. As Christians, we have been given tools to overcome the worries of this life—tools that are rooted in God's Word. This book is a guide to help you lean into God's promises, reminding you that peace is not only possible but promised to those who trust in Him.

The purpose of this book is to provide encouragement, hope, and practical steps for overcoming anxiety. Each chapter is filled with biblical truths, personal reflections, and prayers designed to help you experience the peace that only God can give. As you read, you will be reminded that anxiety does not define you, nor does it have the final say in your life. God's peace, power, and presence are greater than any fear you face.

Understanding Anxiety: A Biblical Perspective

Anxiety is not a new issue. Even in biblical times, people wrestled with fear, worry, and uncertainty. The Bible is filled with accounts of individuals who faced overwhelming circumstances yet found peace and victory through God. Understanding anxiety from a biblical perspective is key to overcoming it.

In the Sermon on the Mount, Jesus spoke directly to the issue of worry. He asked a poignant question:

"Can any one of you by worrying add a single hour to your life?" (Matthew 6:27)

Jesus acknowledged that worry is a natural response to life's challenges, but He also offered a solution: trust in God. He taught His followers to seek first the kingdom of God and trust Him for provision, peace, and purpose (Matthew 6:33). Anxiety often stems from focusing on the things we cannot control. Yet, Jesus redirects our focus to the One who is in control, inviting us to trade worry for trust.

The Bible also assures us that God understands our struggles. In Philippians 4:6-7, Paul writes:

"Do not be anxious about anything, but in every situation, by prayer and petition, with thanksgiving, present your requests to God. And the peace of God, which transcends all understanding, will guard your hearts and your minds in Christ Jesus."

This passage is a cornerstone for anyone dealing with anxiety. It reminds us that prayer is a powerful antidote to worry. When we bring our concerns to God, we experience a peace that transcends human understanding—a peace that guards both our hearts and our minds.

Anxiety, at its core, is a battle of the mind. The enemy uses fear to disrupt our focus and weaken our faith. However, God's Word equips us to fight back. Scriptures like Philippians 4:6-7 and Matthew 6:25-34 serve as reminders that God cares deeply about us and our

needs. He is faithful to provide, and His peace is available to all who seek Him.

Key Scriptures: A Foundation for Peace

Two key scriptures form the foundation for this book, offering hope and guidance as we confront anxiety:

Philippians 4:6-7: "Do not be anxious about anything, but in every situation, by prayer and petition, with thanksgiving, present your requests to God. And the peace of God, which transcends all understanding, will guard your hearts and your minds in Christ Jesus."

This passage encourages us to replace worry with prayer and gratitude. It teaches us that when we trust God with our concerns, He responds by giving us peace.

Matthew 6:25-34: "Therefore I tell you, do not worry about your life, what you will eat or drink; or about your body, what you will wear. Is not life more than food, and the body more than clothes? Look at the birds of the air; they do not sow or reap or store away in barns, and yet your heavenly Father feeds them. Are you not much more valuable than they? Can any one of you by worrying add a single hour to your life?"

In this passage, Jesus reminds us of God's care for His creation. If God provides for the birds of the air and the flowers of the field, how much more will He care for us? This scripture challenges us to trust God completely, knowing that He sees our needs and is faithful to meet them.

These verses lay the groundwork for the journey we will take in this book. They remind us that anxiety is not our identity, and peace is not out of reach. As we dive into each chapter, we will explore practical ways to apply these truths to our daily lives.

An Invitation to Begin the Journey

As you begin this journey, remember that overcoming anxiety is not a one-time event but a daily process of choosing to trust God. It's about learning to rely on Him in every situation and allowing His peace to guard your heart and mind. This book is not just a collection of advice; it's a guide to experiencing the transformative power of God's Word in your life.

Whether you are facing a specific situation that causes anxiety or you struggle with a constant undercurrent of worry, this book is for you. Each chapter is designed to equip you with the tools you need to fight anxiety, renew your mind, and walk in the peace of God. Through Scriptures, reflections, and prayers, you will find encouragement to keep going—even when anxiety feels overwhelming.

Let this book be a reminder that God is bigger than your fears. His promises are true, His presence is constant, and His peace is available to you today. Together, we will explore how to anchor your life in His Word, overcome anxiety, and find the lasting peace that comes from trusting in Him.

Chapter 1: What is Anxiety? A Biblical Perspective

Understanding Anxiety

Anxiety is one of the most common struggles people face, but it is not new. The Bible addresses worry, fear, and distress throughout its pages. Anxiety can manifest as a restless mind, physical tension, or even feelings of despair. It may stem from uncertainty about the future, overwhelming responsibilities, or a lack of control. However, as Christians, we are invited to view anxiety through the lens of faith and trust in God.

In 1 Kings 19, we read about Elijah, a prophet who experienced deep anxiety and despair. After a great victory over the prophets of Baal, Elijah fled in fear for his life. He sat under a broom tree, overwhelmed and praying for God to take his life. Yet, in Elijah's weakest moment, God met him with compassion. He provided food, rest, and reassurance, reminding Elijah that he was not alone. This story reminds us that even the strongest people can face anxiety—and that God's care is always available to us.

The Root of Anxiety

Anxiety is often rooted in fear, whether it's fear of failure, fear of the unknown, or fear of losing control. These fears can cloud our trust in God and distort our perception of His sovereignty. The enemy uses fear to distract us from

God's promises, but Scripture reminds us repeatedly not to fear because God is with us.

Key Scripture:

"For God has not given us a spirit of fear, but of power and of love and of a sound mind." (2 Timothy 1:7)

This verse assures us that fear and anxiety are not from God. Instead, He gives us strength, love, and a peaceful mind. By focusing on His promises, we can combat the lies that anxiety whispers to us.

Biblical Examples of Anxiety

David: In the Psalms, David often poured out his fears to God. He did not hide his anxiety but brought it before the Lord, finding strength in His presence.

"When anxiety was great within me, your consolation brought me joy." (Psalm 94:19)

Martha: In Luke 10:38-42, Martha was "worried and upset about many things" as she prepared to host Jesus. Jesus gently corrected her, reminding her to prioritize being with Him over being consumed by tasks.

Jesus in Gethsemane: Even Jesus experienced intense anguish in the Garden of Gethsemane. He prayed fervently, surrendering His will to the Father and finding peace in God's plan (Matthew 26:36-46).

These examples teach us that anxiety is not sinful in itself but an opportunity to draw closer to God.

God's Invitation to Rest

God understands our struggles and invites us to find rest in Him. Jesus' words in Matthew 11:28-30 are a balm for anxious hearts:

"Come to me, all you who are weary and burdened, and I will give you rest. Take my yoke upon you and learn from me, for I am gentle and humble in heart, and you will find rest for your souls. For my yoke is easy and my burden is light."

This passage reminds us that we don't have to carry our burdens alone. Jesus invites us to exchange our anxiety for His peace.

Practical Steps to Face Anxiety

Acknowledge Your Feelings: It's okay to admit when you're feeling anxious. God wants you to bring your concerns to Him honestly.

Pray and Meditate on Scripture: Use the Word of God as your weapon against fear. Memorize verses that speak to your specific worries.

Seek God's Presence: Spend time in worship and quiet reflection, allowing God's peace to fill your heart.

Surround Yourself with Support: Share your struggles with trusted friends or mentors who can pray with you and encourage you.

Daily Scriptures to Meditate On

Isaiah 41:10: "So do not fear, for I am with you; do not be dismayed, for I am your God. I will strengthen you and help you; I will uphold you with my righteous right hand."

Philippians 4:6-7: "Do not be anxious about anything, but in every situation, by prayer and petition, with thanksgiving, present your requests to God. And the peace of God, which transcends all understanding, will guard your hearts and your minds in Christ Jesus."

Psalm 34:4: "I sought the Lord, and he answered me; he delivered me from all my fears."

Prayer: Finding Peace in God:

Heavenly Father, I come before You with an anxious heart. I acknowledge my fears and worries, but I trust in Your sovereignty and love. You are my refuge and strength, a very present help in trouble. Help me to cast my burdens on You and to rest in Your peace that surpasses understanding. Guide me each day to focus on Your promises and to trust in Your plan. Thank you for your faithfulness and unfailing love. In Jesus' name, Amen.

Chapter 2: Trusting in God's Sovereignty

Introduction

One of the greatest challenges of dealing with anxiety is the feeling of being out of control. Fear thrives in uncertainty, and anxiety often stems from the "what ifs" of life—questions about our future, health, finances, relationships, and purpose. The antidote to this sense of helplessness is found in a simple yet profound truth: God is sovereign. He is in control of all things, and nothing happens outside of His knowledge or will. Trusting in God's sovereignty is foundational for overcoming anxiety, as it reminds us that we can rest in the hands of the One who holds all things together.

What is God's Sovereignty?

The sovereignty of God means that He has supreme authority and control over all creation. Nothing happens without His knowledge or permission. He governs the universe with wisdom, love, and justice. This truth is repeated throughout Scripture:

"The Lord has established his throne in heaven, and his kingdom rules over all." (Psalm 103:19)

"He is before all things, and in him all things hold together." (Colossians 1:17)

God's sovereignty does not mean that life will be free from challenges or pain. Rather, it means that even in the midst of difficulties, God is working all things together for good for those who love Him (Romans 8:28). His plans are greater than we can comprehend, and His purposes are always for His glory and our ultimate good.

The Connection Between Trust and Peace

Trusting in God's sovereignty brings peace because it shifts the burden of control from us to Him. When we trust that God is in control, we no longer need to carry the weight of trying to figure everything out. This is the essence of Proverbs 3:5-6:

"Trust in the Lord with all your heart and lean not on your own understanding; in all your ways submit to him, and he will make your paths straight."

When anxiety arises, it often stems from our desire to control situations that are beyond our ability to manage. Trusting God means surrendering that control and believing that He will guide us, even when we don't understand the path ahead.

Biblical Examples of Trusting God's Sovereignty

Joseph: Betrayed by his brothers, sold into slavery, and unjustly imprisoned, Joseph's life was filled with circumstances that could have caused anxiety. Yet, he trusted in God's sovereignty. At the end of his journey, Joseph declared to his brothers:

"You intended to harm me, but God intended it for good to accomplish what is now being done, the saving of many lives." (Genesis 50:20)

Job: Job faced unimaginable loss—his family, health, and wealth were all taken from him. Yet, he trusted God's sovereignty, saying:

"The Lord gave and the Lord has taken away; may the name of the Lord be praised." (Job 1:21)

Jesus: In the Garden of Gethsemane, Jesus prayed to the Father, saying:

"My Father, if it is possible, may this cup be taken from me. Yet not as I will, but as you will." (Matthew 26:39) Even in the face of the cross, Jesus trusted the Father's plan, knowing that it would bring redemption to the world.

These examples remind us that trusting God's sovereignty doesn't mean life will be easy, but it does mean that we can have peace amid life's storms.

Practical Steps to Trust in God's Sovereignty

Acknowledge God's Control: Begin each day by reminding yourself that God is in control. Surrender your plans to Him and ask for His guidance.

"Commit your way to the Lord; trust in him and he will do this." (Psalm 37:5)

Meditate on God's Promises: Fill your mind with Scriptures that remind you of God's faithfulness and sovereignty. "And we know that in all things God works for the good of those who love him, who have been called according to his purpose." (Romans 8:28)

Surrender Your Fears: Write down the things that are causing you anxiety and intentionally release them to God in prayer. Trust Him to handle what you cannot control.

Seek God's Presence: Spend time in worship, prayer, and stillness, allowing God to remind you of His power and love.

Daily Scriptures to Meditate On

Isaiah 41:10: "So do not fear, for I am with you; do not be dismayed, for I am your God. I will strengthen you and help you; I will uphold you with my righteous right hand."

Psalm 46:1-2: "God is our refuge and strength, an ever-present help in trouble. Therefore, we will not fear, though the earth give way and the mountains fall into the heart of the sea."

Matthew 6:26: "Look at the birds of the air; they do not sow or reap or store away in barns, and yet your heavenly Father feeds them. Are you not much more valuable than they?"

Prayer: Trusting God's Sovereignty:

Heavenly Father, I acknowledge that You are sovereign over all things. Nothing happens outside of Your knowledge or control. When I feel overwhelmed by the uncertainties of life, help me to trust in Your perfect plan. Teach me to surrender my fears and anxieties to You, knowing that You are working all things together for my good. Strengthen my faith and remind me of Your presence in every moment. Thank You for being my refuge and strength. In Jesus' name, Amen.

Chapter 3: Be Still and Know

Introduction

In a world that glorifies busyness and constant motion, the idea of being still can feel foreign. Anxiety thrives in chaos, feeding on the noise and distractions that fill our lives. Yet, God calls us to a different rhythm—a rhythm of rest, stillness, and trust. The phrase "Be still and know that I am God" is not just a comforting verse; it is an invitation to pause, reflect, and experience His peace amid life's storms.

This chapter focuses on the biblical principle of stillness and how embracing God's presence can help us overcome anxiety. Being still does not mean inactivity or passivity; it means surrendering control and allowing God to work in and through us.

The Call to Stillness

The call to stillness is found in Psalm 46:10:

"Be still, and know that I am God; I will be exalted among the nations, I will be exalted in the earth."

This verse was written in a time of turmoil, reminding God's people to cease striving and trust in His sovereignty. Stillness is not about doing nothing but about quieting our hearts and minds to focus on God. It is a deliberate act of trust that acknowledges His power and faithfulness.

In Exodus 14:14, Moses told the Israelites as they faced the Red Sea:

"The Lord will fight for you; you need only to be still."

At that moment, the Israelites were trapped between the sea and the Egyptian army. Anxiety must have been overwhelming, yet God called them to trust Him and remain still, demonstrating that He alone would deliver them.

The Power of Being Still

Stillness Renews Our Strength: Anxiety drains us physically, emotionally, and spiritually. Stillness allows us to rest and be renewed in God's presence. Isaiah 40:31 reminds us:

"But those who hope in the Lord will renew their strength. They will soar on wings like eagles; they will run and not grow weary, they will walk and not be faint."

Stillness Focuses Our Minds on God: Anxiety often causes our minds to race with thoughts of "what if?" Being still helps us redirect our focus from our problems to God's promises. Colossians 3:2 encourages us:

"Set your minds on things above, not on earthly things."

Stillness Invites God's Peace: When we intentionally pause to be still, we create space for God's peace to fill our hearts. Philippians 4:7 promises:

"And the peace of God, which transcends all understanding, will guard your hearts and your minds in Christ Jesus."

Practical Ways to Practice Stillness

Quiet Time with God: Set aside time each day to be alone with God. Read Scripture, pray, and sit in silence, allowing His presence to calm your heart.

Example: Begin your morning with 10 minutes of silence, meditating on a verse like Psalm 46:10.

Worship and Reflection: Play worship music and focus on the lyrics. Use this time to reflect on God's goodness and faithfulness.

Breath Prayers: Practice breathing deeply and repeating a simple prayer, such as "Lord, I trust You" or "You are my peace."

Journaling: Write down your worries and release them to God. Reflect on how He has been faithful in the past and trust Him for the future.

Sabbath Rest: Dedicate a day or a few hours each week to rest from work and focus on God. Use this time to recharge spiritually and emotionally.

Biblical Examples of Finding Peace in Stillness

Jesus in the Storm: In Mark 4:35-41, Jesus calmed a raging storm while His disciples panicked. His command, "Peace! Be still!", not only calmed the sea but also reminded the disciples of His authority over all things.

Mary at Jesus' Feet: In Luke 10:38-42, Mary sat at Jesus' feet, listening to His words, while Martha was "worried and upset about many things." Jesus commended Mary for choosing what was better—the stillness of being in His presence.

Elijah and the Gentle Whisper: In 1 Kings 19, Elijah experienced God's presence not in the powerful wind, earthquake, or fire, but in a gentle whisper. This reminds us that God often speaks in the quiet moments when we are still and attentive.

Daily Scriptures to Meditate On

Psalm 46:10: "Be still, and know that I am God; I will be exalted among the nations, I will be exalted in the earth."

Exodus 14:14: "The Lord will fight for you; you need only to be still."

Isaiah 26:3: "You will keep in perfect peace those whose minds are steadfast because they trust in you."

Prayer: Resting in God's Presence:

Heavenly Father, I come to You weary and burdened by the weight of anxiety. Teach me to be still in Your presence and to trust in Your sovereignty. Help me to quiet my mind and heart so that I can hear Your gentle whisper. Fill me with Your peace that surpasses all understanding and remind me that You are fighting my battles. Thank You for being my refuge and strength. In Jesus' name, Amen.

Chapter 4: Casting Your Cares

Introduction

Anxiety often feels like carrying a heavy burden—one that weighs us down and drains our strength. The Bible acknowledges this reality and offers a solution: casting our cares on God. The act of casting is intentional. It requires us to take the weight we are carrying and place it in the hands of the One who is strong enough to carry it for us.

This chapter explores the biblical command to cast our cares on God and how doing so leads to freedom from anxiety. When we surrender our worries to God, we exchange our burdens for His peace.

What Does It Mean to Cast Your Cares?

The term "cast" means to throw or release something intentionally. In the context of anxiety, casting your cares means taking your worries, fears, and burdens and giving them to God. This act requires trust and humility, as it acknowledges that we cannot handle life's challenges on our own.

Key Scripture:

"Cast all your anxiety on him because he cares for you." (1 Peter 5:7)

This verse reminds us that God is not indifferent to our struggles. He cares deeply for us and invites us to bring our concerns to Him. The word "all" is significant—there is no care too small or too big for God to handle.

Why Do We Struggle to Cast Our Cares?

Despite God's invitation, many of us struggle to release our anxieties to Him. Here are some common reasons:

Fear of Losing Control: We often believe that worrying gives us some measure of control over a situation. In reality, it only magnifies our stress.

Doubt in God's Care: Anxiety can cause us to question whether God truly cares about our struggles. Yet Scripture assures us of His compassion.

"The Lord is gracious and righteous; our God is full of compassion." (Psalm 116:5)

Habit of Self-Reliance: Many of us are used to solving problems on our own, but God calls us to depend on Him.

"Trust in the Lord with all your heart and lean not on your own understanding." (Proverbs 3:5)

Overcoming these barriers requires us to deepen our trust in God and believe that He is both willing and able to carry our burdens.

How to Cast Your Cares on God

Identify Your Burdens: Begin by recognizing what is causing your anxiety. Write down your worries or speak them aloud in prayer. This step helps you bring clarity to what you are carrying.

Surrender in Prayer: Take your list of worries to God in prayer. Tell Him exactly what you are feeling and ask Him to take control.

"Do not be anxious about anything, but in every situation, by prayer and petition, with thanksgiving, present your requests to God." (Philippians 4:6)

Replace Worry with Trust: After surrendering your cares to God, choose to trust Him. This may involve meditating on Scriptures that affirm His faithfulness.

"Commit your way to the Lord; trust in him and he will do this." (Psalm 37:5)

Release Repeatedly: Casting your cares is not a one-time act but a continual process. Whenever anxiety resurfaces, remind yourself to release it to God again.

Biblical Examples of Casting Cares

Hannah's Prayer: In 1 Samuel 1, Hannah was deeply distressed over her inability to have children. She poured out her heart to God in prayer, casting her burden on Him. Afterward, her face was no longer downcast, showing the peace that comes from surrendering to God.

Jesus in Gethsemane: In Matthew 26:36-46, Jesus experienced intense anguish as He faced the cross. He cast His cares on the Father, praying, "My Father, if it is possible, may this cup be taken from me. Yet not as I will, but as you will." His prayer of surrender led to peace and strength to fulfill His mission.

Paul and Silas in Prison: In Acts 16:25-26, Paul and Silas cast their cares on God through prayer and worship, even while in prison. Their trust in God's sovereignty led to miraculous deliverance.

The Peace That Follows Surrender

When we cast our cares on God, we experience His peace—a peace that is not dependent on circumstances but rooted in His character. Philippians 4:7 reminds us:

"And the peace of God, which transcends all understanding, will guard your hearts and your minds in Christ Jesus."

God's peace acts as a shield, protecting us from the onslaught of anxiety and fear. It allows us to rest in the assurance that He is in control.

Daily Scriptures to Meditate On

1 Peter 5:7: "Cast all your anxiety on him because he cares for you."

Matthew 11:28-30: "Come to me, all you who are weary and burdened, and I will give you rest. Take my yoke upon you and learn from me, for I am gentle and humble in heart, and you will find rest for your souls. For my yoke is easy and my burden is light."

Psalm 55:22: "Cast your cares on the Lord and he will sustain you; he will never let the righteous be shaken."

Prayer: Releasing Your Burdens:

Heavenly Father, I come before You with the burdens that weigh heavily on my heart. I acknowledge that I cannot carry them on my own. Today, I choose to cast my cares on You, knowing that You care for me deeply. Help me to release control and trust in Your sovereignty. Fill me with Your peace and remind me that You are always with me. Thank you for carrying my burdens and sustaining me. In Jesus' name, Amen.

Chapter 5: Guarding Your Heart and Mind

Introduction

Anxiety often begins in the mind, where negative thoughts and fears can take root and grow. Left unchecked, these thoughts can influence our emotions, actions, and even our faith. The Bible emphasizes the importance of guarding our hearts and minds because they are the wellsprings of our spiritual lives. In Proverbs 4:23, we are reminded:

"Above all else, guard your heart, for everything you do flows from it."

This chapter focuses on the importance of protecting our hearts and minds against the lies of the enemy and the overwhelming weight of anxiety. It will provide practical and spiritual tools to help you replace fear with truth and peace.

The Connection Between the Heart and Mind

The heart and mind are deeply interconnected in Scripture. The heart often represents our emotions, desires, and will, while the mind refers to our thoughts, reasoning, and beliefs. Together, they shape how we respond to life's challenges.

When anxiety takes hold, it impacts both our heart and mind. Worry fills our thoughts, leading to feelings of fear and unease. This is why the Bible urges us to guard both:

"And the peace of God, which transcends all understanding, will guard your hearts and your minds in Christ Jesus."

(Philippians 4:7)

This verse shows us that God's peace is a protective force. It stands guard over our inner being, shielding us from the attacks of fear and doubt.

The Importance of Guarding Your Heart

Protecting What You Allow In: Your heart is like a garden; whatever you plant there will grow. If you allow negativity, fear, or lies to enter, they will take root. On the other hand, planting seeds of God's truth will produce peace and faith.

"Do not conform to the pattern of this world, but be transformed by the renewing of your mind." (Romans 12:2)

Filtering Your Influences: Anxiety can often be fueled by what we consume—news, social media, or negative conversations. Guarding your heart means being intentional about the influences you allow into your life.

Focusing on God's Promises: The enemy wants to fill your heart with fear, but God calls you to fill it with His promises. Meditating on His Word strengthens your heart and reminds you of His faithfulness.

The Importance of Guarding Your Mind

1. Taking Thoughts Captive: Anxiety often begins with a single thought that spirals into a web of fear. The Bible teaches us to take control of our thoughts:

"We take captive every thought to make it obedient to Christ." (2 Corinthians 10:5)

When anxious thoughts arise, ask yourself: Does this align with God's truth? Replace lies with Scriptures that affirm God's power and care.

Renewing Your Mind: Transforming your mind is an ongoing process. It involves replacing worldly thinking with godly wisdom and aligning your thoughts with God's truth.

"Set your minds on things above, not on earthly things." (Colossians 3:2)

Resisting the Enemy's Lies: Anxiety is one of the enemy's favorite tools. He whispers lies like, "You're not enough" or

"God won't come through for you." Guarding your mind means standing firm against these lies with the truth of God's Word:

"Submit yourselves, then, to God. Resist the devil, and he will flee from you." (James 4:7)

Practical Steps to Guard Your Heart and Mind

Meditate on Scripture Daily: Fill your mind with God's Word to crowd out negative thoughts. Consider memorizing verses that specifically address anxiety and peace.

Pray Without Ceasing: Keep an ongoing conversation with God throughout your day. When anxious thoughts arise, immediately bring them to Him in prayer.

"Pray continually." (1 Thessalonians 5:17)

Practice Gratitude: Gratitude shifts your focus from what is wrong to what is right. It reminds you of God's faithfulness and blessings.

"Give thanks in all circumstances; for this is God's will for you in Christ Jesus." (1 Thessalonians 5:18)

Set Healthy Boundaries: Protect your heart by setting boundaries in relationships, media consumption, and activities that may contribute to anxiety.

Surround Yourself with Encouragement: Spend time with people who build you up and point you to Christ. A supportive community can help guard your heart and mind.

Biblical Examples of Guarding the Heart and Mind

Daniel's Resolve: In Daniel 1, Daniel resolved not to defile himself with the king's food, choosing instead to honor God. His intentional decision to guard his heart resulted in God's favor and peace, even in a foreign land.

Jesus in the Wilderness: When Jesus was tempted by Satan (Matthew 4:1-11), He guarded His mind by quoting Scripture. His reliance on God's Word serves as an example for us to combat lies with truth.

Paul's Confidence: Despite being imprisoned, Paul demonstrated peace and joy. His letters, including Philippians, show how he guarded his heart and mind through prayer, thanksgiving, and trust in God's plan.

Daily Scriptures to Meditate On

> Proverbs 4:23: "Above all else, guard your heart, for everything you do flows from it."

Philippians 4:7: "And the peace of God, which transcends all understanding, will guard your hearts and your minds in Christ Jesus."

Isaiah 26:3: "You will keep in perfect peace those whose minds are steadfast because they trust in you."

Romans 12:2: "Do not conform to the pattern of this world, but be transformed by the renewing of your mind."

Prayer: Guarding Your Heart and Mind:

Heavenly Father, I come to You seeking Your protection over my heart and mind. Teach me to guard my thoughts and emotions with the truth of Your Word. Help me to take every thought captive and align it with Christ. Protect me from the lies of the enemy and fill my heart with Your peace. May my mind be renewed daily as I meditate on Your promises. Thank You for being my refuge and strength. In Jesus' name, Amen.

Chapter 6: Renewing Your Mind

Introduction

Anxiety often begins with the thoughts we allow to take root in our minds. These thoughts, whether they stem from fear, doubt, or insecurity, can spiral into overwhelming worry if left unchecked. The Bible teaches us that the mind is a powerful battleground, and the key to overcoming anxiety lies in renewing our minds with the truth of God's Word.

Renewing your mind is not a one-time event but a daily process of transforming your thoughts and aligning them with God's promises. In this chapter, we'll explore the importance of renewing your mind, practical steps to do so, and how this process can lead to lasting peace.

The Power of the Mind

The mind is where beliefs are formed, decisions are made, and emotions are influenced. When anxiety takes hold of your thoughts, it can a ect every area of your life. This is why the Bible emphasizes the importance of guarding and renewing your mind:

"Do not conform to the pattern of this world, but be transformed by the renewing of your mind. Then you will be able to test and approve what God's will is—his good, pleasing and perfect will." (Romans 12:2)

Renewing your mind transforms the way you think, shifting your perspective from worldly fear to godly trust. It enables you to see challenges through the lens of faith and respond with confidence in God's plan.

Why Do We Need to Renew Our Minds?

Combat Negative Thinking: Anxiety often feeds on negative and repetitive thoughts. If these thoughts are not replaced with truth, they can dominate your mind and emotions.

"For as he thinks in his heart, so is he." (Proverbs 23:7)

Overcome Lies from the Enemy: The enemy uses lies to fuel anxiety, whispering doubts about God's goodness, provision, and love. Renewing your mind helps you identify and reject these lies.

"You are of your father the devil... there is no truth in him." (John 8:44)

Align Your Thoughts with God's Truth: Renewing your mind helps you focus on God's promises rather than your fears. It replaces worry with trust and peace.

"Set your minds on things above, not on earthly things." (Colossians 3:2)

Practical Steps to Renew Your Mind

Meditate on Scripture: Fill your mind with God's Word. Choose verses that address anxiety and read, memorize, and meditate on them daily.

Example: Meditate on Isaiah 26:3: "You will keep in perfect peace those whose minds are steadfast, because they trust in you."

Take Every Thought Captive: Identify anxious or negative thoughts and replace them with truth. Ask yourself, "Does this thought align with God's Word?"

"We take captive every thought to make it obedient to Christ." (2 Corinthians 10:5)

Pray for Renewal: Ask God to transform your mind and help you focus on His truth. Prayer invites the Holy Spirit to guide your thoughts.

"Create in me a pure heart, O God, and renew a steadfast spirit within me." (Psalm 51:10)

Speak Life Over Yourself: Words have power. Speak Scriptures and affirmations over yourself to declare God's promises.

Example: "I have the mind of Christ" (1 Corinthians 2:16).

Limit Negative Influences: Be mindful of what you expose your mind to, such as news, social media, or conversations that fuel anxiety. Focus on what uplifts and encourages you.

"Finally, brothers and sisters, whatever is true, whatever is noble, whatever is right, whatever is pure, whatever is lovely, whatever is admirable—if anything is excellent or praiseworthy—think about such things." (Philippians 4:8)

Cultivate Gratitude: Gratitude shifts your focus from what's wrong to what's right. Write down daily blessings and thank God for them.

"Give thanks in all circumstances; for this is God's will for you in Christ Jesus." (1 Thessalonians 5:18)

Biblical Examples of Renewed Minds

The Apostle Paul: Paul faced numerous hardships—imprisonment, persecution, and danger—yet his mind was renewed by focusing on Christ. His letters are filled with joy and hope despite his circumstances.

"I have learned the secret of being content in any and every situation, whether well fed or hungry, whether living in plenty or in want." (Philippians 4:12)

Joshua: When Joshua was called to lead the Israelites, God commanded him to meditate on His Word day and night to stay strong and courageous.

"Keep this Book of the Law always on your lips; meditate on it day and night, so that you may be careful to do everything written in it." (Joshua 1:8)

Jesus: In the wilderness, Jesus countered every temptation from Satan with Scripture, demonstrating the power of a mind rooted in God's Word.

"It is written: 'Man shall not live on bread alone, but on every word that comes from the mouth of God.'" (Matthew 4:4)

The Result of a Renewed Mind

A renewed mind leads to peace, clarity, and confidence in God's plan. It transforms your perspective, enabling you to see challenges as opportunities to trust God. As Philippians 4:7 promises, God's peace will guard your heart and mind when you focus on Him.

"You will keep in perfect peace those whose minds are steadfast because they trust in you." (Isaiah 26:3)

Renewing your mind also equips you to encourage others. As you experience the transformation that comes from focusing on God, you can share His peace with those around you.

Daily Scriptures to Meditate On

Romans 12:2: "Do not conform to the pattern of this world, but be transformed by the renewing of your mind."

Philippians 4:8: "Whatever is true, whatever is noble, whatever is right, whatever is pure... think about such things."

2 Timothy 1:7: "For God has not given us a spirit of fear, but of power and of love and of a sound mind."

Prayer: Renewing Your Mind:

Heavenly Father, I come to You seeking the renewal of my mind. Help me to focus on Your truth and reject the lies that fuel my anxiety. Teach me to take every thought captive and align it with Christ. Fill my mind with what is noble, pure, and praiseworthy, and give me the strength to meditate on Your Word daily. Thank You for the peace that comes from a renewed mind. In Jesus' name, Amen.

Chapter 7: The Power of Praise

Introduction

Anxiety has a way of making us feel trapped—stuck in our worries, overwhelmed by uncertainties, and paralyzed by fear. But one of the most powerful ways to break free from anxiety is through praise. Praise shifts our focus from our problems to God's greatness. It reminds us of who God is and what He has done, filling our hearts with faith instead of fear.

Throughout Scripture, we see how praise not only brings joy but also serves as a powerful weapon against anxiety, oppression, and spiritual warfare. This chapter explores how cultivating a lifestyle of praise can help us overcome worry and experience the peace of God.

Why is Praise So Powerful?

Praise Shifts Your Focus Anxiety magnifies problems, but praise magnifies God. When we worship, we stop focusing on what's wrong and start focusing on the One who is in control.

"Oh, magnify the Lord with me, and let us exalt his name together!" (Psalm 34:3)

Praise Invites God's Presence The Bible tells us that God dwells in the praises of His people. When we worship, His presence fills our hearts, bringing peace.

"Yet you are holy, enthroned on the praises of Israel." (Psalm 22:3, ESV)

Praise Defeats the Enemy. Praise is a spiritual weapon. The enemy wants to keep you in a place of worry, but praising God silences fear and discouragement.

"Out of the mouth of babes and nursing infants you have ordained strength, because of Your enemies, that You may silence the enemy and the avenger." (Psalm 8:2)

Praise Strengthens Your Faith When you remind yourself of God's faithfulness through praise, your faith grows stronger, making it easier to trust Him in every circumstance.

"I will remember the deeds of the Lord; yes, I will remember your miracles of long ago." (Psalm 77:11)

Biblical Examples of the Power of Praise

Paul and Silas in Prison (Acts 16:25-26) Paul and Silas were wrongly imprisoned, yet instead of worrying or complaining, they began praising God. As they worshipped, a miraculous earthquake shook the prison, opening the doors and setting them free. Their praise not only changed their situation but also led to the salvation of the jailer and his family. "About midnight, Paul and Silas were praying and singing hymns to God, and the other prisoners were listening to them. Suddenly, there was such a violent earthquake that the foundations of the prison were shaken." (Acts 16:25-26)

Jehoshaphat's Victory (2 Chronicles 20:21-22) When King Jehoshaphat faced a vast army, instead of fighting with weapons, he sent worshippers ahead of the soldiers. As they praised God, He caused confusion in the enemy's camp, leading to victory without a single battle.

"As they began to sing and praise, the Lord set ambushes against the men of Ammon and Moab and Mount Seir who were invading Judah, and they were defeated." (2 Chronicles 20:22)

David's Psalms of Deliverance David, often overwhelmed by fear and distress, turned to praise as his weapon against anxiety. In Psalm 34, written during a time of danger, he declares:

"I sought the Lord, and he answered me; he delivered me from all my fears." (Psalm 34:4) David's life teaches us that praising God in distress brings peace and deliverance.

How to Use Praise to Overcome Anxiety

Sing Worship Songs When anxiety rises, turn on worship music and sing aloud. Music has the power to shift the atmosphere of your heart and mind.

Declare God's Goodness Aloud. Speak words of praise over your life, declaring God's faithfulness.

Example: "God, You are my refuge and strength! You are in control, and I trust you completely!"

Write Down Testimonies of God's Faithfulness, keep a journal of answered prayers, and moments when God has come through for you. Reviewing them will encourage you during anxious times.

Praise in Advance. Don't wait until the problem is solved—praise God before the breakthrough comes, demonstrating your trust in Him.

Read and Pray the Psalms. Many Psalms are filled with praises to God in the middle of difficult situations. Reading and praying them can encourage your heart.

Daily Scriptures to Meditate On

Psalm 34:1: "I will bless the Lord at all times; His praise shall continually be in my mouth."

Isaiah 61:3: "To bestow on them a crown of beauty instead of ashes, the oil of joy instead of mourning, and a garment of praise instead of a spirit of despair."

Philippians 4:4: "Rejoice in the Lord always. I will say it again: Rejoice!"

Psalm 42:11: "Why, my soul, are you downcast? Why so disturbed within me? Put your hope in God, for I will yet praise him, my Savior and my God."

Prayer: Releasing Anxiety Through Praise:

Heavenly Father, I choose to praise You in the midst of my anxiety. You are greater than my worries, stronger than my fears, and more powerful than my struggles. I exalt You above my circumstances and declare Your goodness over my life. Fill my heart with joy and peace as I focus on You. Help me to develop a habit of praise, trusting that You are always in control. Thank You for Your faithfulness and for the peace that comes when I worship You. In Jesus' name, Amen.

Chapter 8: Living One Day at a Time

Introduction

One of the greatest sources of anxiety is worrying about the future. The unknown can feel overwhelming, and the "what ifs" of life can consume our thoughts. Jesus knew that anxiety often stems from focusing too much on tomorrow, which is why He instructed His followers to take life one day at a time.

In Matthew 6:34, Jesus gives us a simple yet powerful command:

"Therefore, do not worry about tomorrow, for tomorrow will worry about itself. Each day has enough trouble of its own."

Living one day at a time doesn't mean ignoring responsibilities or failing to plan. Instead, it means trusting God for today and believing that He will provide for tomorrow. This chapter explores how to embrace the present moment, trust God's daily provision, and find peace by letting go of tomorrow's worries.

Why Do We Worry About the Future?

Fear of the Unknown: Not knowing what will happen can make us feel out of control, leading to worry about our finances, relationships, health, and purpose.

Desire for Security We want to feel safe and prepared, but anxiety tricks us into believing that worrying will somehow protect us.

Lack of Trust in God's Timing. When answers don't come as quickly as we'd like, we may doubt whether God will come through.

Comparing Our Lives to Others: Seeing others succeed can make us anxious about whether we are "falling behind" in life.

All of these anxieties distract us from the fact that God is already in our future, and He is more than capable of taking care of us.

Jesus' Teaching on Worry and Daily Trust

In Matthew 6:25-34, Jesus addresses our natural tendency to worry. He reminds us that if God provides for the birds of the air and the flowers of the field, how much more will He provide for His children?

"Look at the birds of the air; they do not sow or reap or store away in barns, and yet your heavenly Father feeds them. Are you not much more valuable than they?" (Matthew 6:26)

This passage is a call to trust God fully. Birds don't stress about tomorrow—they live moment by moment, trusting their Creator to provide. Jesus calls us to do the same.

"But seek first his kingdom and his righteousness, and all these things will be given to you as well." (Matthew 6:33)

Rather than spending our energy worrying, we are called to seek God first and trust that He will take care of the rest.

Biblical Examples of Trusting God Daily

Manna in the Wilderness (Exodus 16:4-5) When the Israelites were in the desert, God provided manna each day. They could only gather what they needed for that day—any extra would spoil. This was a lesson in daily trust:

"Then the Lord said to Moses, 'I will rain down bread from heaven for you. The people are to go out each day and gather enough for that day.'" (Exodus 16:4) Just as God provided for the Israelites one day at a time, He will provide for us.

Elijah and the Widow (1 Kings 17:8-16) During a famine, God sent Elijah to a widow who had only enough flour and oil for one last meal. Yet when she trusted God, her supply never ran out.

"The jar of flour was not used up and the jug of oil did not run dry, in keeping with the word of the Lord spoken by Elijah." (1 Kings 17:16) This story reminds us that God provides exactly what we need, exactly when we need it.

Jesus Teaching His Disciples to Pray (Matthew 6:11) In the Lord's Prayer, Jesus taught us to ask for "daily bread," emphasizing our need for daily dependence on God.

"Give us today our daily bread." (Matthew 6:11) Jesus didn't say "Give us a year's supply" but "Give us today"—a reminder to trust God each day.

How to Live One Day at a Time

Start Each Day with Prayer. Begin each morning by committing the day to God. Pray for wisdom, strength, and peace to face whatever comes.

Practice Gratitude: Focus on today's blessings rather than tomorrow's uncertainties. Write down things you're grateful for each day.

Let Go of Tomorrow's Worries. When anxious thoughts about the future arise, remind yourself of Jesus' words:

"Do not worry about tomorrow, for tomorrow will worry about itself." (Matthew 6:34)

Trust God's Provision. Remind yourself that God has always provided for you in the past and will continue to do so in the future.

Be Present in the Moment. Enjoy time with loved ones, focus on today's tasks, and appreciate the small joys in life.

Daily Scriptures to Meditate On

Matthew 6:34: "Therefore do not worry about tomorrow, for tomorrow will worry about itself."

Philippians 4:6-7: "Do not be anxious about anything, but in every situation, by prayer and petition, with thanksgiving, present your requests to God."

Psalm 118:24: "This is the day that the Lord has made; let us rejoice and be glad in it."

Lamentations 3:22-23: "Because of the Lord's great love we are not consumed, for his compassions never fail. They are new every morning; great is your faithfulness."

Prayer: Trusting God for Today:

Heavenly Father, I come before You with the worries of my heart. I confess that I often focus too much on tomorrow instead of trusting You for today. Help me to live one day at a time, knowing that You are already in my future. Give me the faith to rely on Your daily provision and the peace to rest in Your promises. Teach me to seek You first and to let go of anxiety about the unknown. Thank You for being my provider, my sustainer, and my peace. In Jesus' name, Amen.

Chapter 9: Walking in Faith, Not Fear

Introduction

Fear and faith cannot coexist. One will always overpower the other. When we allow fear to dominate our thoughts, anxiety takes hold. But when we choose to walk in faith, we experience the peace that comes from trusting God completely.

Many times, anxiety stems from fear of the unknown, fear of failure, or fear of losing control. But the Bible reminds us that faith is the antidote to fear. In 2 Corinthians 5:7, Paul encourages believers to:

"Walk by faith, not by sight."

Faith is not about having all the answers or knowing exactly how things will turn out. It's about trusting God even when we don't see the whole picture. This chapter will help you understand what it means to walk in faith and how trusting God can replace fear with confidence and peace.

Why Does Fear Attack Our Faith?

1. The Enemy Uses Fear as a Weapon

Satan knows that fear can cripple our faith. He whispers lies that make us doubt God's promises.

"The thief comes only to steal and kill and destroy." (John 10:10) 2. Fear Thrives on the Unknown

When we can't see the future, we often assume the worst. But faith reminds us that God is already in our future. "For I know the plans I have for you, declares the Lord, plans to prosper you and not to harm you, plans to give you hope and a future." (Jeremiah 29:11)

Fear Focuses on the Problem, Not the Solution

Anxiety makes our problems seem bigger than God, but faith reminds us that God is bigger than our problems. "Is anything too hard for the Lord?" (Genesis 18:14)

What Does It Mean to Walk in Faith?

Faith is Trusting God Even When You Don't Understand

Abraham left his home without knowing where he was going. He trusted that God would guide him step by step.

"By faith, Abraham obeyed when he was called to go out to a place that he was to receive as an inheritance. And he went out, not knowing where he was going." (Hebrews 11:8)

Faith is Believing God's Word Over Your Feelings

Feelings change, but God's Word remains the same. When fear tells you "This is too much," faith says, "With God, all things are possible" (Matthew 19:26).

Faith is Stepping Forward Even When You're Afraid

Faith doesn't mean you never feel fear. It means you don't let fear control you. Peter walked on water because he trusted Jesus, even though the storm was raging.

"Then Peter got down out of the boat, walked on the water, and came toward Jesus." (Matthew 14:29)

Faith is Declaring Victory Before You See It

Faith is speaking what God has promised before you see it come to pass. Joshua and the Israelites marched around Jericho, praising God before the walls fell.

"By faith, the walls of Jericho fell after the army had marched around them for seven days." (Hebrews 11:30)

Biblical Examples of Walking in Faith Instead of Fear

David Facing Goliath (1 Samuel 17:45-47)

While everyone else was afraid of Goliath, David had faith that God would give him victory. He declared:

The battle is the Lord's, and he will give all of you into our hands."

The Woman with the Issue of Blood (Mark 5:25-34)

This woman had been sick for 12 years. Despite her suffering, she believed that if she could just touch Jesus'

robe, she would be healed. Her faith brought her healing.
3. Shadrach, Meshach, and Abednego (Daniel 3:16-18)

They refused to bow to an idol, even though they faced being thrown into a fiery furnace. They told the king:

"Our God, whom we serve, is able to deliver us from the burning fiery furnace, and He will deliver us out of your hand,

O, king." Their faith led to a miraculous deliverance!

How to Walk in Faith Daily

Speak Faith-Filled Words

Fear speaks doubt, but faith speaks God's promises. Instead of saying, "I'm too weak," say, "The Lord is my strength" (Psalm 28:7).

Replace Worry with Worship

When you feel anxious, start praising God. Worship shifts your focus from fear to faith.

Trust God's Timing

Anxiety often comes from wanting immediate answers. Faith reminds us that God's timing is perfect. "Wait for the Lord; be strong and take heart and wait for the Lord." (Psalm 27:14)

Keep Moving Forward Even when you're afraid, keep taking steps of faith.

"For we live by faith, not by sight." (2 Corinthians 5:7)

Daily Scriptures to Meditate On

2 Timothy 1:7 – "For God has not given us a spirit of fear, but of power and of love and of a sound mind."

Isaiah 41:10 – "So do not fear, for I am with you; do not be dismayed, for I am your God. I will strengthen you and help you."

Hebrews 11:1 – "Now faith is confidence in what we hope for and assurance about what we do not see."

Joshua 1:9 – "Be strong and courageous. Do not be afraid; do not be discouraged, for the Lord your God will be with you wherever you go."

Prayer: Choosing Faith Over Fear:

Heavenly Father, I surrender my fears to You. I confess that sometimes I allow anxiety to overshadow my faith. But today, I choose to trust You. Help me to walk in faith, knowing that You are in control. Strengthen my heart when I feel afraid and remind me of Your promises. I declare that fear has no power over me because I am a child of God. Fill me with boldness, confidence, and peace as I take steps of faith each day. In Jesus' name, Amen.

Chapter 10: God's Promises in Times of Trouble

Introduction

When anxiety strikes, it can feel as though the weight of the world is pressing down on you. Fear whispers that you are alone, that things will never get better, or that you don't have the strength to make it through. But as believers, we have something the world does not—God's unshakable promises.

The Bible is filled with promises of protection, provision, peace, and victory for those who trust in God. These promises remind us that no matter what we face, we are never alone. When we hold onto His Word, we replace anxiety with confidence, fear with faith, and despair with hope.

This chapter explores God's promises in times of trouble and how to stand firm on His Word even in life's most difficult moments.

Why Are God's Promises Important?

God's Promises Give Us Peace

Anxiety thrives in uncertainty. But when we focus on God's promises, we are reminded that He is in control.

"You will keep in perfect peace those whose minds are steadfast because they trust in you." (Isaiah 26:3)

God's Promises Never Fail

Human promises can be broken, but God is always faithful.

"Not one of all the Lord's good promises to Israel failed; everyone was fulfilled." (Joshua 21:45)

God's Promises Give Us Strength

When we feel weak, His Word strengthens us and gives us courage.

"But those who hope in the Lord will renew their strength. They will soar on wings like eagles." (Isaiah 40:31)

God's Promises for Different Struggles

When You Feel Overwhelmed

"When you pass through the waters, I will be with you; and when you pass through the rivers, they will not sweep over you. When you walk through the fire, you will not be burned." (Isaiah 43:2) Promise: God will be with you in every storm, and He will bring you through it.

When You Feel Alone

"Be strong and courageous. Do not be afraid or terrified, for the Lord your God goes with you; He will never leave you nor forsake you." (Deuteronomy 31:6)

Promise: God is always with you, even when you feel forgotten.

When You Are Afraid

"For God has not given us a spirit of fear, but of power and of love and of a sound mind." (2 Timothy 1:7)
Promise: Fear does not come from God—He gives you power and peace.

When You Are Worried About the Future

"For I know the plans I have for you, declares the Lord, plans to prosper you and not to harm you, plans to give you hope and a future." (Jeremiah 29:11)

Promise: God already has a good plan for your life—trust in His timing.

When You Are Struggling Financially

"And my God will meet all your needs according to the riches of his glory in Christ Jesus." (Philippians 4:19)
Promise: God will always provide what you need.

When You Need Strength to Keep Going

"I can do all things through Christ who gives me strength." (Philippians 4:13) Promise: God will give you the strength to endure every challenge.

When You Feel Like Giving Up

"The Lord is close to the brokenhearted and saves those who are crushed in spirit." (Psalm 34:18) Promise: God is near you in your hardest moments.

How to Stand on God's Promises

Read and Meditate on Scripture Daily

Fill your heart with God's Word so that His promises are the first thing that comes to mind when anxiety arises. "Let the word of Christ dwell in you richly." (Colossians 3:16)

Declare God's Promises Out Loud

Speaking Scripture over your life is a way of a irming God's truth and rejecting fear.

"Death and life are in the power of the tongue." (Proverbs 18:21)

Pray God's Promises Back to Him

When you pray, use Scripture to remind yourself (and the enemy) of what God has promised.

Example: "Lord, You promised that You would never leave me (Deuteronomy 31:6), so I trust that You are with me even in this moment."

Write Down Promises to Remember

Keep a journal of God's promises and reflect on how He has fulfilled them in your life.

Surround Yourself with Encouragement

Connect with other believers who can remind you of God's faithfulness when you feel discouraged.

Biblical Examples of People Who Stood on God's Promises

Abraham – Trusting God's Promise of a Son

God promised Abraham that he would have a son, but he had to wait 25 years for that promise to be fulfilled. "Yet he did not waver through unbelief regarding the promise of God but was strengthened in his faith and gave glory to God." (Romans 4:20)

Lesson: Even when God's promises take time, they will come to pass.

Moses – Trusting God's Promise to Deliver Israel

Moses led the Israelites out of Egypt based on God's promise, even though Pharaoh resisted.

"The Lord will fight for you; you need only to be still." (Exodus 14:14)

Lesson: God always keeps His word, even when obstacles stand in the way.

Mary – Trusting God's Promise About Jesus

Mary believed God when the angel told her she would give birth to the Savior.

"Blessed is she who has believed that the Lord would fulfill his promises to her!" (Luke 1:45) Lesson: Faith in God's promises brings blessings.

Daily Scriptures to Meditate On

Psalm 91:4 – "He will cover you with his feathers, and under his wings, you will find refuge; his faithfulness will be your shield and rampart."

Hebrews 10:23 – "Let us hold unswervingly to the hope we profess, for he who promised is faithful."

Romans 8:28 – "And we know that in all things God works for the good of those who love him."

2 Corinthians 1:20 – "For no matter how many promises God has made, they are 'Yes' in Christ.

Prayer: Trusting God's Promises:

Heavenly Father, thank You for the promises in Your Word. When I feel anxious, remind me that Your promises are true and that You are always faithful. Help me to trust You completely, even when I cannot see the way ahead. I stand on Your Word and declare that fear has no place in my life. Thank you for being my provider, protector, and peace. In Jesus' name, Amen.

Chapter 11: Breaking Free from the Spirit of Fear

Introduction

Fear is one of the greatest weapons the enemy uses against believers. It paralyzes, limits, and robs us of the peace and joy that God has promised. Fear can manifest in many ways—fear of failure, fear of rejection, fear of the unknown, or fear of loss. When fear takes hold, it can lead to anxiety, doubt, and spiritual bondage.

However, as children of God, we are not meant to live in fear. The Bible tells us that fear is not from God:

"For God has not given us a spirit of fear, but of power and of love and of a sound mind." (2 Timothy 1:7)

This chapter will help you recognize the spirit of fear, understand its effects, and learn how to break free from its grip so that you can walk in confidence and peace.

Understanding the Spirit of Fear

What is the Spirit of Fear?

Fear is not just an emotion; it can also be a spiritual force that seeks to control and oppress. The enemy uses fear to:

Keep us from fulfilling God's calling.

Make us doubt God's promises.

Steal our peace and joy.

Keep us in a state of constant worry and anxiety.

The Bible refers to fear as a spirit—something that influences and affects us. But God has given us power over it.

"You did not receive a spirit of slavery to fall back into fear, but you have received the Spirit of adoption as sons, by whom we cry, 'Abba! Father!'" (Romans 8:15)

How Does Fear Gain Power Over Us?

Through Negative Thoughts

Fear begins in the mind. If we dwell on fearful thoughts, they will grow and take control. "For as he thinks in his heart, so is he." (Proverbs 23:7)

Through Past Trauma or Pain

Fear can take root from past experiences of failure, rejection, or loss.

Through Lies from the Enemy

The devil uses fear as a tool to make us doubt God's promises.

"He is a liar and the father of lies." (John 8:44)

Through Lack of Trust in God

Fear thrives where faith is weak. The more we trust in God, the less room fear has to grow.

How to Break Free from the Spirit of Fear

Identify and Expose the Fear

Write down the fears that are controlling you.

Ask yourself: "Where is this fear coming from?"

Fear loses its power when it is brought into the light.

Replace Fear with the Truth of God's Word

Fear tells you that you are alone, but God's Word says:

"Never will I leave you; never will I forsake you." (Hebrews 13:5) Fear says you will fail, but God says:

"I can do all things through Christ who strengthens me." (Philippians 4:13)

Pray Against the Spirit of Fear

Use prayer as a weapon to break fear's hold over you.

Speak God's promises over your life and command fear to leave.

Declare Your Authority Over Fear

Jesus has given you authority over fear and anxiety.

"I have given you authority to trample on snakes and scorpions and to overcome all the power of the enemy." (Luke 10:19)

Speak out loud: "I reject the spirit of fear in Jesus' name. I walk in power, love, and a sound mind!"

Surround Yourself with Faith-Building Encouragement

Listen to sermons, worship music, and testimonies that remind you of God's faithfulness.

Spend time with believers who will pray for you and encourage you.

Take Steps of Faith

Fear wants you to stay stuck, but faith moves forward even when it's afraid.

Start doing the things fear tells you that you can't do.

Biblical Examples of Overcoming Fear

Gideon – From Fearful to Mighty Warrior (Judges 6:11-16)

Gideon was afraid and hiding when God called him. But God saw him not as he was, but as who he could become—a mighty warrior.

"The Lord is with you, mighty warrior." (Judges 6:12)

Lesson: God sees past our fear and calls us to something greater.

Peter Walking on Water (Matthew 14:22-33)

When Peter focused on Jesus, he walked on water. But when he focused on the storm, fear made him sink.

"Immediately Jesus reached out his hand and caught him. 'You of little faith,' he said, 'why did you doubt?'" (Matthew 14:31)

Lesson: Keeping our eyes on Jesus allows us to overcome fear.

The Israelites at the Red Sea (Exodus 14:13-14)

The Israelites were trapped between Pharaoh's army and the Red Sea. Fear told them they would die, but God made a way.

"The Lord will fight for you; you need only to be still." (Exodus 14:14)

Lesson: God is always in control, even when fear tells us there is no way out.

Daily Scriptures to Meditate On

2 Timothy 1:7 – "For God has not given us a spirit of fear but of power, love, and a sound mind."

Isaiah 41:10 – "Do not fear, for I am with you; do not be dismayed, for I am your God."

Psalm 34:4 – "I sought the Lord, and he answered me; he delivered me from all my fears."

Romans 8:15 – "You did not receive a spirit of slavery to fall back into fear."

John 14:27 – "Peace I leave with you; my peace I give you. Do not let your hearts be troubled and do not be afraid."

Prayer: Breaking Free from Fear:

Heavenly Father, I come before You in Jesus' name, declaring freedom from the spirit of fear. I reject every lie that fear has spoken into my life, and I stand on the truth of Your Word. You have not given me a spirit of fear but of power, love, and a sound mind. Fill me with Your peace and boldness. Help me to walk in faith and not be ruled by fear. Thank You for Your presence, for Your promises, and for Your unfailing love. In Jesus' name, Amen.

Chapter 12: Seeking God's Peace Daily

Introduction

Peace is one of the most precious gifts that God offers us. Yet, in a world filled with uncertainty, fear, and constant distractions, maintaining peace can feel impossible. Anxiety fights to dominate our hearts and minds, making us restless and overwhelmed. But God's peace is not dependent on our circumstances—it is a supernatural peace that surpasses understanding.

Jesus promised us this peace:

"Peace I leave with you; my peace I give you. I do not give to you as the world gives. Do not let your hearts be troubled and do not be afraid." (John 14:27)

God's peace is available every single day, but we must learn how to seek it, receive it, and walk in it. This chapter will guide you in making God's peace a daily reality in your life.

What is God's Peace?

There are two kinds of peace mentioned in the Bible:

Peace with God – This happens when we surrender our lives to Christ. Because of Jesus' sacrifice, we are reconciled with God.

"Therefore, since we have been justified through faith, we have peace with God through our Lord Jesus Christ." (Romans 5:1)

The Peace of God – This is an ongoing peace that guards our hearts and minds, no matter what we face.

"And the peace of God, which transcends all understanding, will guard your hearts and your minds in Christ Jesus." (Philippians 4:7)

The peace of God is what keeps us from being consumed by worry, doubt, and fear. It is a gift, but we must actively seek and protect it.

Why Do We Lose Our Peace?

Focusing on Problems Instead of God

When we magnify our problems, we minimize God's power.

"You will keep in perfect peace those whose minds are steadfast because they trust in you." (Isaiah 26:3)

Trying to Control Everything

When we hold onto control, we become anxious. Surrendering to God brings peace.

"Trust in the Lord with all your heart and lean not on your own understanding." (Proverbs 3:5)

Listening to Negative Thoughts

The enemy whispers lies that create fear. We must replace them with truth.

"We take captive every thought to make it obedient to Christ." (2 Corinthians 10:5)

Busyness and Distraction

A cluttered life often leads to a cluttered heart. We must make time for God's presence. "Be still, and know that I am God." (Psalm 46:10)

How to Seek God's Peace Daily

Start Your Day with God

Before checking your phone or worrying about the day, spend time in prayer and the Word. Pray: "Lord, fill me with Your peace today."

Give Your Worries to God

Make it a daily habit to cast your cares on Him.

"Cast all your anxiety on him because he cares for you." (1 Peter 5:7)

Stay in a Posture of Gratitude

Gratitude shifts your focus from worry to God's goodness.

"Give thanks in all circumstances." (1 Thessalonians 5:18)

Guard Your Thoughts

Fill your mind with God's truth instead of negativity.

"Whatever is true, noble, right, pure, lovely, admirable—think about such things." (Philippians 4:8)

Rest in God's Presence

Spend time in worship, prayer, and stillness to refresh your spirit.

"The Lord gives strength to his people; the Lord blesses his people with peace." (Psalm 29:11)

Trust God's Timing

Anxiety often comes from impatience. Trust that God's plan is perfect.

"Wait for the Lord; be strong and take heart and wait for the Lord." (Psalm 27:14)

Surround Yourself with Peace

Limit negative influences (news, social media, toxic conversations).

Spend time with people who speak life and faith into you.

Biblical Examples of Seeking God's Peace

Jesus Sleeping in the Storm (Mark 4:35-41)

While the disciples panicked, Jesus slept during a storm. He knew His Father was in control.

"Peace! Be still!" (Mark 4:39)

Lesson: When we trust God, we can have peace even in the storms of life.

Mary at Jesus' Feet (Luke 10:38-42)

Martha was stressed and anxious, but Mary chose peace by sitting at Jesus' feet.

"Martha, Martha, you are worried and upset about many things, but only one thing is needed." (Luke 10:41-42) Lesson: Peace comes from spending time with Jesus, not from doing more.

Paul's Peace in Prison (Philippians 4:11-13)

Even in prison, Paul had peace and contentment because he trusted God.

"I have learned the secret of being content in any and every situation." (Philippians 4:12) Lesson: Peace is not about circumstances; it's about trust in God.

Daily Scriptures to Meditate On

John 14:27 – "Peace I leave with you; my peace I give you."

Philippians 4:6-7 – "Do not be anxious about anything, but in every situation, by prayer and petition, with thanksgiving, present your requests to God."

Isaiah 26:3 – "You will keep in perfect peace those whose minds are steadfast because they trust in you."

Psalm 4:8 – "In peace, I will lie down and sleep, for you alone, Lord, make me dwell in safety."

Prayer: Seeking God's Peace Daily:

Heavenly Father, I long to walk in Your peace each day. Help me to trust You instead of worrying about what I cannot control. I release my anxieties to You and receive Your peace that surpasses understanding. Teach me to rest in Your presence, focus on Your promises, and guard my heart against distractions. Thank You for being my refuge, my protector, and my source of peace. In Jesus' name, Amen.

Chapter 13: Encouragement Through Community

Introduction

Anxiety often makes us feel isolated. It whispers lies that no one understands, that we must handle our struggles alone, or that reaching out for help is a sign of weakness. But God never intended for us to face life's battles in isolation. He created us for community, knowing that we thrive when we are surrounded by godly encouragement, prayer, and support.

The Bible emphasizes the importance of fellowship and encourages believers to bear one another's burdens:

"Carry each other's burdens, and in this way you will fulfill the law of Christ." (Galatians 6:2)

God often provides peace and strength through the people He places in our lives. This chapter explores how community plays a vital role in overcoming anxiety and how to build relationships that uplift and encourage.

Why Is Community Important?

We Are Not Meant to Carry Burdens Alone

Anxiety grows in isolation. But when we share our struggles, we find support, wisdom, and strength.

"Two are better than one, because they have a good return for their labor: If either of them falls down, one can help the other up." (Ecclesiastes 4:9-10)

Encouragement Strengthens Our Faith

Being around faith-filled believers reminds us of God's promises and helps us stay strong during difficult times. "Therefore, encourage one another and build each other up." (1 Thessalonians 5:11)

Accountability Helps Us Stay Focused on God

Anxiety can cause us to drift away from spiritual disciplines. A strong community keeps us accountable in our walk with God.

"And let us consider how we may spur one another on toward love and good deeds." (Hebrews 10:24-25)

Praying with Others Brings Breakthrough

When we pray together, God moves powerfully in our lives.

"For where two or three gather in my name, there am I with them." (Matthew 18:20)

Biblical Examples of Strength in Community

Moses, Aaron, and Hur (Exodus 17:10-13)

When Moses held up his sta , Israel prevailed in battle. But when he grew tired, Aaron and Hur held up his arms so that he could continue. Their support brought victory.

Lesson: When we are weak, godly friends strengthen us.

Ruth and Naomi (Ruth 1:16-17)

Ruth refused to leave Naomi's side, saying:

"Where you go I will go, and where you stay I will stay." (Ruth 1:16)

Ruth's loyalty brought blessings to both of them.

Lesson: God places people in our lives to walk with us through difficult seasons.

The Early Church (Acts 2:42-47)

The early Christians prayed together, shared what they had, and supported one another. As a result, they were filled with joy and saw God work in miraculous ways.

Lesson: A strong community strengthens our faith and brings joy.

How to Build a Godly Community

Be Intentional About Fellowship

Make time to connect with others at church, Bible study groups, or small groups.

"Do not give up meeting together, as some are in the habit of doing." (Hebrews 10:25)

Surround Yourself with Encouraging People

Be with people who speak life, faith, and hope into you. Avoid relationships that fuel fear and negativity.

"Walk with the wise and become wise." (Proverbs 13:20)

Share Your Struggles Honestly

Don't be afraid to be vulnerable with trusted friends.

"Confess your sins to each other and pray for each other so that you may be healed." (James 5:16)

Pray with Others Regularly

Find a prayer partner or join a group that prays together.

"They all joined together constantly in prayer." (Acts 1:14)

Be a Source of Encouragement

Sometimes, the best way to receive encouragement is to give it.

"A generous person will prosper; whoever refreshes others will be refreshed." (Proverbs 11:25)

What to Do If You Feel Alone

Sometimes, despite our efforts, we may feel like we don't have a strong community. If that's you, here are some steps you can take:

Pray for God to Bring the Right People into Your Life

Ask Him to connect you with godly friends and mentors.

Join a Church or Small Group

If you're not already involved in a Bible study, prayer group, or ministry, this is a great place to start.

Reach Out to Others First

Sometimes, others are waiting for you to make the first move. Start a conversation, invite someone to co ee, or check in on someone.

Stay Patient and Open

Building meaningful relationships takes time. Keep seeking, and God will provide the right connections.

Daily Scriptures to Meditate On

Galatians 6:2 – "Carry each other's burdens, and in this way, you will fulfill the law of Christ."

Hebrews 10:24-25 – "Let us consider how we may spur one another on toward love and good deeds."

Proverbs 27:17 – "As iron sharpens iron, so one person sharpens another."

Romans 12:10 – "Be devoted to one another in love. Honor one another above yourselves."

Prayer: Finding Strength in Community:

Heavenly Father, thank You for creating us to live in fellowship with one another. Help me to build strong, faith-filled relationships that encourage and strengthen me. Lead me to the right people, and help me to be a source of encouragement to others as well. When I feel alone, remind me that You are always with me. Surround me with a godly community and fill my heart with peace. In Jesus' name, Amen.

Chapter 14: Victory Through the Word of God

Introduction

The Bible is more than just a book—it is a weapon against fear, anxiety, and spiritual attacks. When anxiety overwhelms, God's Word provides clarity, strength, and peace. It is our spiritual sword, equipping us to stand firm against the lies of the enemy.

Hebrews 4:12 describes the power of Scripture:

"For the word of God is alive and active. Sharper than any double-edged sword, it penetrates even to dividing soul and spirit, joints and marrow; it judges the thoughts and attitudes of the heart."

This chapter will explore how immersing yourself in Scripture can help you fight anxiety and how you can use God's Word to claim victory over fear and doubt.

Why Is the Word of God So Powerful?

The Word of God is Truth

Anxiety is often fueled by lies about your worth, your future, and God's care for you. Jesus declared: "Then you will know the truth, and the truth will set you free." (John 8:32) When you replace anxious thoughts with God's truth, you break free from fear.

The Word of God Builds Faith

Fear weakens faith, but Scripture strengthens it.

"Faith comes from hearing, and hearing through the word of Christ." (Romans 10:17) When you read God's Word, your trust in Him grows stronger.

The Word of God is a Spiritual Weapon

The Bible is called the Sword of the Spirit, meant for battling anxiety and fear.

"Take up the sword of the Spirit, which is the word of God." (Ephesians 6:17)

When the enemy attacks your mind with anxiety, declare Scripture to fight back.

Biblical Examples of Victory Through God's Word

Jesus Defeating Satan with Scripture (Matthew 4:1-11)

When Satan tempted Jesus, He didn't argue—He responded with Scripture.

"It is written: 'Man shall not live on bread alone, but on every word that comes from the mouth of God.'" (Matthew 4:4) Lesson: The Word of God is the most powerful weapon against fear and temptation.

David's Confidence in God's Promises (Psalm 119:105)

David constantly turned to God's Word for guidance and strength. "Your word is a lamp to my feet and a light to my path." (Psalm 119:105) Lesson: The Bible provides direction when anxiety clouds your mind.

Paul Encouraging Believers to Stand Firm (Ephesians 6:10-17)

Paul reminds us that we are in a spiritual battle and must arm ourselves with the Word.

"Put on the full armor of God, so that you can take your stand against the devil's schemes." (Ephesians 6:11) Lesson: God's Word protects and strengthens us in spiritual warfare.

How to Use God's Word to Overcome Anxiety

Speak Scripture Over Your Life

Declare God's promises out loud when anxiety arises.

Example: If you feel overwhelmed, say:

"I can do all things through Christ who strengthens me." (Philippians 4:13)

Memorize Key Verses

Store God's Word in your heart so you can recall it in moments of fear.

"I have hidden your word in my heart that I might not sin against you." (Psalm 119:11)

Write Down Verses That Speak to You

Keep a journal or note cards with Scriptures to encourage you throughout the day.

Read the Bible Daily

Set aside time every day to meditate on God's truth and renew your mind.

Pray Scripture Over Your Situation

Use Bible verses in your prayers to claim God's promises over your life. Example:

"Lord, You said that You will never leave me nor forsake me (Deuteronomy 31:6). I trust in Your presence and strength."

Key Scriptures for Overcoming Anxiety

Isaiah 41:10 – "So do not fear, for I am with you; do not be dismayed, for I am your God. I will strengthen you and help you; I will uphold you with my righteous right hand."

Philippians 4:6-7 – "Do not be anxious about anything, but in every situation, by prayer and petition, with thanksgiving, present your requests to God. And the peace of God, which transcends all understanding, will guard your hearts and your minds in Christ Jesus."

Psalm 34:4 – "I sought the Lord, and he answered me; he delivered me from all my fears."

John 14:27 – "Peace I leave with you; my peace I give you. I do not give to you as the world gives. Do not let your hearts be troubled and do not be afraid."

Romans 8:37 – "No, in all these things we are more than conquerors through Him who loved us."

Daily Declaration: Speaking God's Word Over Your Life

Repeat these declarations daily to strengthen your faith and fight against anxiety:

 "I am a child of God, and fear has no hold on me." (Romans 8:15) "God has not given me a spirit of fear, but of power, love, and a sound mind." (2 Timothy 1:7) "The Lord is my refuge and my fortress; I will trust in Him." (Psalm 91:2) "I am strong and courageous, for the Lord is with me wherever I go." (Joshua 1:9) "I have the mind of Christ, and my thoughts are in alignment with God's truth." (1 Corinthians 2:16)

Prayer: Claiming Victory Through God's Word:

Heavenly Father, I thank You for the power of Your Word. When anxiety tries to overwhelm me, remind me of Your promises. I declare that Your Word is my foundation, my shield, and my sword against fear. I reject every lie of the enemy and stand firm in the truth that You are with me. Strengthen my heart and fill me with peace as I meditate on Your Word daily. In Jesus' name, Amen.

Chapter 15: Living in Freedom

Introduction

Freedom from anxiety is not just a temporary relief—it is a way of life that God desires for you. Jesus came not just to forgive sins, but to set us free from everything that holds us captive, including fear and anxiety.

"So if the Son sets you free, you will be free indeed." (John 8:36)

Living in freedom means walking daily in the peace, trust, and confidence that comes from knowing God is in control, His promises are true, and His presence is with you always. In this final chapter, we will explore how to maintain victory over anxiety, live in spiritual and emotional freedom, and walk forward in the abundant life that God has planned for you.

What Does It Mean to Live in Freedom?

Freedom is Trusting God Completely

Anxiety often comes from a lack of control, but true freedom comes from surrendering everything to God. "Trust in the Lord with all your heart and lean not on your own understanding." (Proverbs 3:5)

Freedom is Walking in Peace Daily

Living free means that peace becomes your default state, not fear.

"Let the peace of Christ rule in your hearts." (Colossians 3:15)

Freedom is Knowing You Are No Longer a Slave to Fear

You have been set free—fear and anxiety no longer have power over you.

"For you did not receive a spirit of slavery to fall back into fear, but you have received the Spirit of adoption as sons." (Romans 8:15)

How to Maintain Your Freedom from Anxiety

Keep Your Mind Fixed on God

"You will keep in perfect peace those whose minds are steadfast because they trust in you." (Isaiah 26:3) When anxiety tries to creep in, immediately redirect your thoughts back to God's promises.

Use Scripture as Your Daily Weapon

Keep declaring God's Word over your life.

"Take the helmet of salvation and the sword of the Spirit, which is the word of God." (Ephesians 6:17)

Continue Casting Your Cares on God

Anxiety often creeps back in because we start carrying burdens again.

Daily give your worries to God in prayer.

"Cast all your anxiety on him because he cares for you." (1 Peter 5:7)

Surround Yourself with a Strong Community

Stay connected with believers who encourage you and pray for you.

"And let us consider how we may spur one another on toward love and good deeds." (Hebrews 10:24)

Walk in Gratitude and Praise

Gratitude keeps anxiety from taking root in your heart. Praise shifts your focus from worry to worship.

"Give thanks in all circumstances; for this is God's will for you." (1 Thessalonians 5:18)

Speak Life Over Yourself

Reject thoughts of fear and replace them with God's truth.

Declare: "I am free from anxiety because Christ has set me free!" "God is my refuge and strength; I will not fear." "The Lord is my peace and my protector."

Stay Consistent in Prayer and Worship

The more time you spend in God's presence, the more peace you will experience.

"Draw near to God, and He will draw near to you." (James 4:8)

Biblical Examples of Living in Freedom

Paul's Boldness Despite Hardships (Philippians 4:11-13)

Paul faced prison, persecution, and hardship, yet he walked in freedom and peace.

"I have learned the secret of being content in any and every situation... I can do all things through Christ who strengthens me." (Philippians 4:12-13)

The Israelites Entering the Promised Land (Joshua 1:9)

After years of fear and wandering, God told Joshua:

"Be strong and courageous. Do not be afraid; do not be discouraged, for the Lord your God will be with you wherever you go." (Joshua 1:9)

Lesson: Living in freedom means stepping forward in faith.

Peter's Confidence After Being Filled with the Holy Spirit (Acts 2:14-41)

Peter, once afraid and anxious, became bold and fearless after encountering the Holy Spirit.

Lesson: The power of God transforms us from fearful to fearless.

Daily Scriptures to Meditate On

John 8:36 – "So if the Son sets you free, you will be free indeed."

2 Timothy 1:7 – "For God has not given us a spirit of fear but of power, love, and a sound mind."

Romans 8:37 – "No, in all these things we are more than conquerors through Him who loved us."

Psalm 118:6 – "The Lord is with me; I will not be afraid. What can mere mortals do to me?"

Galatians 5:1 – "It is for freedom that Christ has set us free. Stand firm, then, and do not let yourselves be burdened again by a yoke of slavery."

Prayer: Walking in Freedom:

Heavenly Father, I thank You for the freedom I have in Christ. I declare that anxiety, fear, and worry no longer have power over me. I choose to walk in faith, trusting in Your promises and resting in Your peace. Help me to stay grounded in Your Word, surround myself with encouragement, and live a life of praise. I am more than a conqueror through Christ, and I will walk boldly in the freedom You have given me. Thank You for setting me free! In Jesus' name, Amen.

Chapter 16: Spiritual Warfare Against Anxiety

Introduction

Anxiety is not just a mental or emotional battle; it is often a spiritual attack. The enemy seeks to fill our hearts with fear, worry, and doubt to keep us from walking in faith and trusting God. However, as believers, we have been given spiritual weapons to fight against anxiety and fear.

Paul reminds us in Ephesians 6:12:"For our struggle is not against flesh and blood, but against the rulers, against the authorities, against the powers of this dark world and against the spiritual forces of evil in the heavenly realms."

This chapter will guide you in recognizing anxiety as a spiritual battle, equipping you with biblical tools to fight back and walk in victory through Christ. Recognizing the Spiritual Battle

Anxiety often begins in the mind, but its root can be deeply spiritual. The devil wants to:

Distract You from God – Anxiety keeps your focus on problems instead of God's promises.

Weaken Your Faith – Fear and doubt try to diminish your trust in God's goodness.

Steal Your Peace and Joy – The enemy knows that a peaceful believer is a powerful believer.

However, God has given us authority over fear and anxiety. The Bible says:

"Submit yourselves, then, to God. Resist the devil, and he will flee from you." (James 4:7)

When you recognize anxiety as a spiritual battle, you can begin to fight it with the right weapons.

Weapons for Spiritual Warfare Against Anxiety

The Word of God (The Sword of the Spirit)

The Bible is your most powerful weapon against fear.

"For the word of God is alive and active. Sharper than any double-edged sword." (Hebrews 4:12) Speak scriptures of peace and victory over your life.

Prayer and Fasting

Jesus said that some battles require prayer and fasting (Matthew 17:21). Spend time in deep prayer, surrendering your fears to God.

Worship and Praise

Praise confuses the enemy and strengthens your faith.

"He has given me the garment of praise instead of a spirit of despair." (Isaiah 61:3)

The Armor of God (Ephesians 6:10-18)

Put on the helmet of salvation to guard your mind.

Use the shield of faith to block the enemy's attacks.

Biblical Example: Jesus Resisting the Enemy

When Jesus was tempted in the wilderness (Matthew 4:1-11), Satan tried to plant fear, doubt, and lies in His mind. But Jesus resisted the enemy by declaring scripture.

The devil said: "If you are the Son of God, tell these stones to become bread."

Jesus responded: "It is written: 'Man shall not live on bread alone, but on every word that comes from the mouth of God.'"

Lesson: When fear attacks, speak God's truth out loud!

Daily Scriptures to Fight Spiritual Anxiety

2 Corinthians 10:4 – "The weapons we fight with are not the weapons of the world. On the contrary, they have divine power to demolish strongholds."

Isaiah 41:10 – "Do not fear, for I am with you; do not be dismayed, for I am your God."

Romans 8:37 – "No, in all these things we are more than conquerors through Him who loved us."

Prayer: Overcoming Anxiety Through Spiritual Warfare: Heavenly Father, I recognize that

Anxiety is not just a mental struggle but a spiritual battle. I take up the weapons of spiritual warfare and declare victory in Jesus' name. I reject fear, doubt, and worry, and I stand firm on Your promises.

Strengthen me with Your Word, and fill me with Your peace. In Jesus' name, Amen.

Chapter 17: The Role of the Holy Spirit in Overcoming Anxiety

Introduction

Anxiety often arises when we feel lost, uncertain, or powerless. But as believers, we are never alone. The Holy Spirit is our divine Helper, Comforter, and Guide, given to us by God to bring peace, wisdom, and strength in moments of fear and worry.

Jesus Himself promised us the Holy Spirit when He said:

"But the Advocate, the Holy Spirit, whom the Father will send in my name, will teach you all things and will remind you of everything I have said to you. Peace I leave with you; my peace I give you. I do not give to you as the world gives. Do not let your hearts be troubled and do not be afraid." (John 14:26-27)

The peace we need doesn't come from our circumstances but from the presence of the Holy Spirit within us. This chapter will explore how the Holy Spirit helps us combat anxiety, how to develop a deeper relationship with Him, and how to walk daily in the peace He provides.

Who is the Holy Spirit?

The Holy Spirit is the third person of the Trinity—God Himself living within us. He is not a distant force but a personal Helper who empowers, comforts and strengthens us.

He is our Comforter (John 14:16) – He brings peace to our troubled hearts.

He is our Teacher (John 14:26) – He reminds us of God's Word when we feel anxious.

He is our Guide (John 16:13) – He leads us into truth and wisdom.

He is our Strength (Romans 8:26) – He helps us when we feel weak.

How the Holy Spirit Helps Us Overcome Anxiety

The Holy Spirit Brings Supernatural Peace

One of the greatest weapons against anxiety is the peace of God, which the Holy Spirit provides. This is not an ordinary peace—it is supernatural and unshakable.

"The mind governed by the flesh is death, but the mind governed by the Spirit is life and peace."

(Romans 8:6)

"For God is not a God of disorder but of peace." (1 Corinthians 14:33)

When we submit our thoughts and fears to the Holy Spirit, He replaces our anxiety with divine peace that surpasses understanding (Philippians 4:7).

The Holy Spirit Reminds Us of God's Promises

Anxiety thrives on fear, doubt, and lies—but the Holy Spirit reminds us of God's truth. When fear tells you:

"You are alone." → The Holy Spirit reminds you: "I will never leave you nor forsake you." (Hebrews 13:5)

"You won't make it through this." → The Holy Spirit whispers: "I can do all things through Christ who strengthens me." (Philippians 4:13) Jesus said:

"He will teach you all things and will remind you of everything I have said to you." (John 14:26) The Holy Spirit brings scripture to our minds in moments of fear, giving us strength and courage.

The Holy Spirit Strengthens Our Faith

Faith is the opposite of anxiety. When we lack faith, we allow fear to take control. But when we walk in the Spirit, our faith is strengthened.

"I pray that out of His glorious riches, He may strengthen you with power through His Spirit in your inner being." (Ephesians 3:16)

The Holy Spirit builds our spiritual endurance, reminding us that God is faithful even in uncertain times.

The Holy Spirit Helps Us Pray When We Feel Overwhelmed

Sometimes, anxiety leaves us speechless and exhausted. We don't know what to pray, or we feel too weak to pray at all. But the Holy Spirit prays for us and through us.

"In the same way, the Spirit helps us in our weakness. We do not know what we ought to pray for, but the Spirit himself intercedes for us through wordless groans." (Romans 8:26)

Even when you feel too anxious to pray, the Holy Spirit steps in, interceding on your behalf.

How to Invite the Holy Spirit into Your Life Daily

Spend Time in Prayer and Worship

Invite the Holy Spirit to fill your heart and mind each morning.

Pray: "Holy Spirit, guide my thoughts and fill me with peace today."

Read and Meditate on God's Word

The Holy Spirit uses scripture to combat anxiety.

Keep Bible verses about peace near you and read them daily.

Listen for the Holy Spirit's Guidance

Make room for quiet time with God and listen for His gentle leading.

The Holy Spirit often speaks through scripture, worship, and a sense of deep inner peace.

Ask the Holy Spirit to Fill You with Peace

Simply say: "Holy Spirit, I surrender my anxiety to You. Fill me with Your peace."

Biblical Example: The Holy Spirit Strengthens the Early Church

After Jesus' resurrection, the disciples were full of fear and anxiety. They were hiding in a locked room, afraid of persecution. But then, something miraculous happened—the Holy Spirit came upon them at Pentecost (Acts 2).

Suddenly, these fearful men became bold preachers of the Gospel. Peter, who once denied Jesus out of fear, stood up and proclaimed the Word with courage and power.

Lesson:

The Holy Spirit turns fear into faith and anxiety into boldness!

Daily Scriptures to Invite the Holy Spirit's Peace

John 14:26-27 – "The Holy Spirit... will teach you all things and remind you of everything I have said to you. Peace I leave with you; my peace I give you."

Romans 8:6 – "The mind governed by the Spirit is life and peace." Galatians 5:22 – "The fruit of the Spirit is love, joy, peace, forbearance, kindness, goodness, faithfulness."

2 Timothy 1:7 – "For the Spirit God gave us does not make us timid, but gives us power, love, and self-discipline."

Prayer: Inviting the Holy Spirit to Overcome Anxiety:

Heavenly Father, I invite the Holy Spirit into my heart today. Fill me with Your peace that surpasses all understanding. When anxiety tries to take over, remind me of Your promises. Strengthen my faith, guide my thoughts, and help me to walk in victory. Holy Spirit, be my comforter, my teacher, and my source of strength. I surrender my fears to You and choose to trust in You. In Jesus' name, Amen.

Chapter 18: Prayers and Declarations for Anxiety-Free Living

Introduction

Anxiety thrives in an environment of fear, doubt, and uncertainty. However, God has given us a powerful tool to combat anxiety: prayer and biblical declarations.

Through prayer, we communicate with God, surrendering our fears and receiving His peace. Through declarations, we speak God's truth over our lives, aligning our thoughts with His Word rather than the lies of the enemy.

The Bible tells us:

"Do not be anxious about anything, but in every situation, by prayer and petition, with thanksgiving, present your requests to God. And the peace of God, which transcends all understanding, will guard your hearts and your minds in Christ Jesus." (Philippians 4:6-7)

This chapter will provide specific prayers and declarations you can use daily to replace fear with faith and anxiety with peace.

The Power of Prayer Against Anxiety

Prayer is more than just words—it is an act of surrender and trust. When we bring our worries to God, we allow Him to carry our burdens and replace them with His peace.

Jesus Himself modeled prayer as the solution to worry:

"Cast all your anxiety on Him because He cares for you." (1 Peter 5:7)

"Come to me, all you who are weary and burdened, and I will give you rest." (Matthew 11:28) The more we pray, the more we diminish the power of anxiety over our lives.

Daily Prayers for Overcoming Anxiety

Morning Prayer for Peace

Starting your day with prayer sets the tone for peace and trust in God.

Prayer: "Heavenly Father, as I begin this day, I choose peace over fear. I surrender my anxieties, worries, and uncertainties into Your hands. Fill me with Your presence and guide my thoughts. Let Your Word be my anchor today, and may Your peace guard my heart and mind. In Jesus' name, Amen."

Prayer When Feeling Overwhelmed

Anxiety often creeps in when we feel burdened. This prayer helps release those burdens to God.

Prayer: "Father, I feel overwhelmed by the weight of my worries. Your Word says to cast my cares upon You because You care for me. Right now, I lay every concern at Your feet. I refuse to let anxiety steal my peace. Fill me with Your calm assurance and remind me that You are in control. In Jesus' name, Amen." 3. Prayer for Strength and Courage

When anxiety causes fear, we need to pray for boldness and trust.

Prayer: "Lord, I declare that I am strong and courageous in You. Fear has no power over me because You are my refuge. Remind me that You have not given me a spirit of fear, but of power, love, and a sound mind. Fill me with courage today as I face challenges. In Jesus' name, Amen."

Prayer for Protection from Anxiety Attacks

When sudden waves of anxiety hit, pray for God's protection over your heart and mind.

Prayer: "Heavenly Father, I take authority over every anxious thought in Jesus' name. I put on the full armor of God and declare that my mind is protected by the helmet of salvation. Let Your peace flood my soul and drive out all fear. You are my refuge and strength. I trust in You. Amen."

Nighttime Prayer for Rest and Peace

Anxiety often disrupts sleep, but God's peace brings rest.

Prayer: "Lord, as I lay down to sleep, I trust in Your protection. I reject every anxious thought and choose to dwell in Your presence. Let Your angels watch over me. I rest in Your peace, knowing that You hold tomorrow in Your hands. In Jesus' name, Amen."

The Power of Declarations Over Anxiety

Declarations are faith-filled statements based on God's Word. Speaking these out loud helps to renew our minds and shift our focus from fear to faith.

The Bible tells us:

"Death and life are in the power of the tongue." (Proverbs 18:21)

"Let the weak say, 'I am strong.'" (Joel 3:10)

When we declare God's Word, we align our thoughts and emotions with His truth.

Biblical Declarations to Speak Over Your Life

Declaration of Peace "I declare that God's peace, which surpasses all understanding, guards my heart and mind in Christ Jesus. I reject fear and embrace God's perfect peace." (Philippians 4:7)

Declaration of Trust "I trust in the Lord with all my heart and do not lean on my own understanding. He directs my path, and I will not be afraid." (Proverbs 3:5-6)

Declaration of Strength "I am strong in the Lord and in the power of His might. Fear has no place in my life, for God has given me a spirit of power, love, and a sound mind." (Ephesians 6:10, 2 Timothy 1:7)

Declaration Against Fear "I declare that I am free from fear because the Lord is with me. I will not be shaken, for He is my fortress and deliverer." (Psalm 27:1)

Declaration of Victory Over Anxiety "No weapon formed against me shall prosper. Anxiety and fear have no authority in my life. I am more than a conqueror through Christ!" (Isaiah 54:17, Romans 8:37) How to Incorporate Prayer and Declarations Into Your Daily Life

Start your morning with prayer – Begin each day by giving your worries to God.

Declare God's Word out loud – Speaking truth combats anxious thoughts.

Write down your favorite scriptures – Keep them visible for encouragement.

Pray whenever anxiety arises – Turn every fearful moment into an opportunity to seek God.

End your day with thanksgiving – Thank God for His peace before you sleep.

Biblical Examples of Prayers Bringing Peace

Jesus Praying in the Garden of Gethsemane (Matthew 26:36-39)

Before Jesus faced the cross, He experienced deep distress. He prayed, "My soul is overwhelmed with sorrow to the point of death." But as He prayed, He received strength from the Father.

Lesson: When we feel overwhelmed, prayer brings strength and peace.

Paul's Declaration of Trust (2 Corinthians 12:9-10) Paul faced great hardships, but he declared:

"My grace is sufficient for you, for my power is made perfect in weakness." (2 Corinthians 12:9) Lesson: When we declare God's truth, we find strength in weakness.

Daily Scriptures to Meditate On

Philippians 4:6-7 – "Do not be anxious about anything, but in every situation, by prayer and petition, with thanksgiving, present your requests to God."

Isaiah 41:10 – "So do not fear, for I am with you."

2 Timothy 1:7 – "For the Spirit God gave us does not make us timid, but gives us power, love, and self-discipline."

Psalm 34:4 – "I sought the Lord, and he answered me; he delivered me from all my fears."

Final Prayer: Walking in Victory Over Anxiety:

"Heavenly Father, I thank You that I am free from anxiety through Christ. I choose to pray instead of worry, to declare truth instead of fear, and to trust instead of doubt.

Fill my heart with faith and peace. I stand on Your Word and declare that I am victorious! In Jesus' name, Amen."

Chapter 19: Developing a Lifestyle of Trust

Introduction

Anxiety thrives in uncertainty, and trust is the antidote. Many people only seek God when they feel anxious, but true peace comes from living in a constant state of trust, not just seeking God in moments of crisis.

The Bible calls us to trust in God at all times:

"Trust in the Lord with all your heart and lean not on your own understanding; in all your ways submit to him, and he will make your paths straight." (Proverbs 3:5-6)

This chapter will teach you how to develop trust as a daily lifestyle rather than just a reaction to anxiety. When trust becomes your foundation, peace follows naturally. Why Trusting God is the Key to Overcoming Anxiety

Many people struggle with trust because:

They have been hurt before – Past disappointments make them fear trusting again.

They want to be in control – Fear arises when things feel out of control.

They don't fully understand God's character – Anxiety is fueled by uncertainty about God's plans.

But trusting God is a choice. Even when we don't understand His plans, we can trust His character, knowing He is good, loving, and in control.

"Blessed is the one who trusts in the Lord, whose confidence is in Him." (Jeremiah 17:7)

Steps to Develop a Lifestyle of Trust

Know Who God Is

You can't trust someone you don't know. The more you learn about God's faithfulness in the Bible, the easier it is to trust Him.

He is Faithful – "God is faithful, who has called you into fellowship with his Son, Jesus Christ our

Lord." (1 Corinthians 1:9)

He is Loving – "Give thanks to the Lord, for he is good; his love endures forever." (Psalm 107:1) He is in Control – "I make known the end from the beginning, from ancient times, what is still to come. My purpose will stand." (Isaiah 46:10)

Action Step: Spend time daily reading about God's character in scripture.

Surrender Control to God

Most anxiety comes from fear of the unknown or trying to control outcomes. Trust means letting go and allowing God to take charge.

"Cast your burden on the Lord, and He will sustain you." (Psalm 55:22) Practical Way to Surrender:

Write down everything that's causing anxiety.

Pray over each concern, telling God you trust Him with it.

Physically throw the paper away as a symbol of releasing control.

Choose Faith Over Fear

Fear and faith cannot coexist. The more we trust God, the less power fear has over us.

"When I am afraid, I put my trust in you." (Psalm 56:3)

Faith-building practice: Every time fearful thoughts arise, replace them with:

A scripture about trust (e.g., Isaiah 26:3 – "You will keep in perfect peace those whose minds are steadfast because they trust in You.")

A spoken declaration (e.g., "God is in control, and I trust Him completely!")

Remember God's Past Faithfulness

One of the best ways to build trust is to remember how God has helped you before. Anxiety makes us forget past victories, but trust is built when we reflect on God's goodness.

"I will remember the deeds of the Lord; yes, I will remember your miracles of long ago." (Psalm 77:11)

Action Step: Keep a "God's Faithfulness Journal" where you write down answered prayers and moments where God provided. Review it when you feel anxious.

Biblical Example: Abraham's Journey of Trust

Abraham is called the father of faith because he trusted God even when things didn't make sense.

God told him to leave his home without knowing where he was going (Genesis 12:1).

God promised him a son despite his old age (Genesis 15:6).

God asked him to sacrifice Isaac, but he trusted God would provide (Genesis 22:8).

Each time Abraham trusted God, his faith grew stronger.

Lesson: Trust is built one step at a time. Start trusting God with small things, and your faith will grow.

Daily Scriptures for Trusting God

Psalm 37:5 – "Commit your way to the Lord; trust in him and he will do this."

Isaiah 26:3 – "You will keep in perfect peace those whose minds are steadfast because they trust in You."

Proverbs 3:5-6 – "Trust in the Lord with all your heart and lean not on your own understanding."

Romans 8:28 – "And we know that in all things God works for the good of those who love him."

Prayer: Developing a Lifestyle of Trust:

"Heavenly Father, I want to trust You with my whole heart. Help me to surrender control and rest in Your promises. I choose faith over fear and confidence over anxiety. Remind me daily that You are good, You are faithful, and You are always in control. Teach me to walk in trust and experience Your perfect peace. In Jesus' name, Amen."

Chapter 20: A Final Encouragement - Walking in God's Peace Permanently

Introduction

Overcoming anxiety is not just a one-time event—it is a daily journey of learning to trust God, rest in His promises, and walk in His peace. This final chapter will encourage you to maintain your victory over anxiety and live in God's peace every day.

Jesus promised us permanent peace, not just temporary relief:

"Peace I leave with you; my peace I give you. I do not give to you as the world gives. Do not let your hearts be troubled and do not be afraid." (John 14:27)

The world's peace is based on circumstances—when things are good, we feel peace; when life is uncertain, anxiety creeps in. But God's peace is different. It is an inner peace that remains regardless of circumstances.

This chapter will equip you to walk in God's peace permanently, no matter what challenges you face.

What Does It Mean to Walk in God's Peace?

Walking in peace is not about having a problem-free life. It is about having a heart and mind so anchored in God that fear, worry, and doubt cannot shake you.

Paul described this peace as something beyond human understanding:

"And the peace of God, which transcends all understanding, will guard your hearts and your minds in Christ Jesus." (Philippians 4:7)

To walk in God's peace permanently, we must:

Remain rooted in His Word

Stay in constant communication with Him through prayer

Guard our hearts and minds against anxiety triggers

Live with an attitude of faith and gratitude

How to Maintain Your Victory Over Anxiety

Continue to Trust God Daily

Trusting God is a daily choice. Even when circumstances seem overwhelming, you must make the decision to believe that God is in control.

"You will keep in perfect peace those whose minds are steadfast because they trust in you." (Isaiah 26:3)

Practical Step:

Each morning, declare: "God, I trust You today, no matter what comes my way."

Protect Your Mind from Negative Thoughts

Anxiety often starts in the mind. That's why the Bible teaches us to renew our minds and focus on things that bring peace.

"Do not conform to the pattern of this world, but be transformed by the renewing of your mind."

(Romans 12:2)

"Finally, brothers and sisters, whatever is true, whatever is noble, whatever is right, whatever is pure, whatever is lovely, whatever is admirable—if anything is excellent or praiseworthy—think about such things." (Philippians 4:8)
Practical Step:

Identify and remove negative influences (news, social media, toxic relationships) that trigger anxiety.

Fill your mind with God's truth—memorize and meditate on peaceful scriptures.

Stay Connected to God Through Prayer

Prayer is not just for crisis moments—it is a lifestyle. To walk in continuous peace, you must stay in constant communication with God.

"Pray without ceasing." (1 Thessalonians 5:17)

"Cast all your anxiety on Him because He cares for you." (1 Peter 5:7) Practical Step:

Develop a daily prayer habit (morning, throughout the day, before bed).

When anxiety arises, stop and pray immediately, rather than letting worry grow.

Surround Yourself with Faith-Filled People

Your environment impacts your peace. If you surround yourself with negative, fearful people, their anxiety will rub o on you. Instead, stay connected to faith-filled believers who encourage and uplift you.

"As iron sharpens iron, so one person sharpens another." (Proverbs 27:17)

"Let us consider how we may spur one another on toward love and good deeds." (Hebrews 10:24) Practical Step:

Be part of a Bible study group, church, or prayer community that encourages trust in God. Find an accountability partner who will remind you to walk in faith when fear arises.

Keep an Attitude of Gratitude

Anxiety and gratitude cannot coexist. When you focus on what you are thankful for, it shifts your mind away from fear and worry.

"Give thanks in all circumstances; for this is God's will for you in Christ Jesus." (1 Thessalonians 5:18) Practical Step:

Start a gratitude journal—write down three things you are thankful for every day. When you feel anxious, stop and thank God for His faithfulness.

Biblical Example: Paul's Unshakable Peace

Paul endured shipwrecks, imprisonment, beatings, and persecution—yet he never lost his peace. Why? Because he had complete trust in God.

While in prison, Paul wrote:

"I have learned to be content whatever the circumstances." (Philippians 4:11)

Paul's peace was not based on his circumstances. It was based on his faith in God's goodness.

Lesson:

If Paul could rejoice in prison, we can walk in peace no matter what we face.

Daily Scriptures for Walking in Peace

John 14:27 – "Peace I leave with you; my peace I give you. Do not let your hearts be troubled."

Philippians 4:6-7 – "Do not be anxious about anything… And the peace of God, which transcends all understanding, will guard your hearts."

Isaiah 41:10 – "Do not fear, for I am with you; do not be dismayed, for I am your God."

Colossians 3:15 – "Let the peace of Christ rule in your hearts."

Final Prayer: Walking in God's Peace Permanently:

"Heavenly Father, I thank You that Your peace is not temporary—it is eternal. I choose to walk in Your peace every day. No matter what circumstances I face, I will trust in You. I reject fear, anxiety, and worry, and I embrace Your perfect peace. Guard my heart and mind, and lead me in Your truth. In Jesus' name, Amen."

Final Encouragement: Living a Life Free from Anxiety

As you finish this book, remember:

Anxiety does not define you. God's peace is always available to you. You have the tools to walk in peace permanently.

Whenever anxiety tries to return, go back to God's promises, your prayers, and declarations, and remember:

You are victorious in Christ.

God's peace is yours to walk in daily.

You never have to live in fear again.

Next Steps: How to Keep Growing in Your Faith and Peace

Continue reading and meditating on God's Word.

Stay connected with other believers.

Make prayer and gratitude part of your daily routine.

Remind yourself of God's faithfulness when fear tries to return.

Congratulations! You Have Completed This Journey! 🎉

You now have everything you need to live a life free from anxiety. Keep walking in faith, trusting in God, and living in His peace daily.

Made in the USA
Coppell, TX
14 May 2025

49403180R00070